Parliamentary Elections in Britain

LONDON
HER MAJESTY'S STATIONERY OFFICE

Prepared by
REFERENCE DIVISION
CENTRAL OFFICE OF INFORMATION
LONDON

© *Crown copyright 1978*
First published 1978

101182

· 324.42
CEN

ISBN 011 700977 6

0073891

N.B. *This pamphlet is one of a series produced by the Central Office of Information for British Information Services. To meet requests from inquirers in the United Kingdom, certain pamphlets in the series are being made available on sale from Her Majesty's Stationery Office.*

6

CONTENTS

		Page
INTRODUCTION	.. ..	1
EXTENSION OF THE FRANCHISE ..	.. ..	2
CONSTITUENCIES	.. ..	3
VOTERS AND CANDIDATES	.. ..	5
ELECTORAL PROCEDURE ..	.. ..	8
APPENDICES		
1. The General Election of October 1974 ..	.. ..	17
2. General Election Results 1945–74	.. ..	18
READING LIST ..	.. ..	20

ADDENDUM

Elections to the European Assembly

The European Assembly Elections Act 1978 provides that of the 81 representatives from the United Kingdom to the European Assembly 66 shall be elected in England; 8 in Scotland; 4 in Wales; and 3 in Northern Ireland. Voting will be by the simple majority system in single-member constituencies in Great Britain and the single transferable vote system of proportional representation in one constituency in Northern Ireland. The Assembly constituencies in Great Britain will consist of groupings of United Kingdom parliamentary constituencies. The franchise and conditions for candidature will be the same as for parliamentary elections with the addition that peers will be entitled to stand and to vote. There is no requirement in the Act that candidates should be Members of Parliament.

It has been announced that the first elections of United Kingdom representatives to the Assembly will take place on 7 June 1979.

INTRODUCTION

THE BRITISH system of parliamentary government[1] is sustained by an electorate casting its votes freely at periodic elections which offer a choice between rival candidates, representing, in the great majority of cases, organised political parties of different views. The Government is normally formed from the party which has (or can command the support of) a majority of members of the House of Commons and depends for its continuance in office on maintaining this majority support. The Government is responsible, through the House of Commons, to the electorate as a whole.

A general election, for all seats in the House of Commons, must take place at least every five years, but a Parliament may be and often is dissolved by the Queen, acting on the advice of the Prime Minister, before the end of the full legal term. When a seat falls vacant in the period between general elections (for example, on the death or resignation of a member) a by-election is held.

The simple majority system of voting—by which a candidate is elected if he has a majority vote over the next candidate (although not necessarily an absolute majority over all other candidates)—is used in parliamentary and local government elections, except in local government elections in Northern Ireland which are held under a system of proportional representation.

Questions concerning changes in electoral law are considered periodically by a Speaker's conference consisting of members of the House of Commons. The Prime Minister consults parliamentary party leaders on the terms of reference for the conference and, once these are decided, invites the Speaker of the House of Commons to preside. As with other parliamentary committees, the party composition of the conference reflects that of the House. The proceedings are in private and recommendations are published in the form of letters from the Speaker to the Prime Minister. They are not binding on the Government.

Bills at present before Parliament would provide for elections to new assemblies to be set up in Scotland and Wales. A Bill making provision for the election of British representatives to the Assembly of the European Community completed its passage through Parliament in May. Its main provisions are summarised in the addendum opposite.

---

[1]A description of Parliament is given in COI reference pamphlet *The British Parliament*, R5448.

1

EXTENSION OF THE FRANCHISE

ALTHOUGH the British Parliament dates from the thirteenth century, democratic elections with full adult suffrage are a comparatively recent development, the vote having been extended to all women over 21 in 1928. The first legislation to make the House of Commons more representative came in 1832. Prior to that date property qualifications restricted the vote to a very small minority of the population. Moreover, little redistribution of seats had occurred, in spite of the fact that many people had moved away from rural areas to find employment in the expanding towns created by the Industrial Revolution. The new industrial areas had not received increased representation to take account of their growth, and some had no representation.

The 1832 legislation abolished seats representing areas of virtually no population (the 'rotten boroughs') and distributed them to the more populated areas. The franchise was extended to a wider range of electors but the great majority of the population (including all women) remained without voting rights.

In 1867 the Representation of the People Act extended the franchise further by adding nearly a million voters to the electorate. Further redistribution again transferred some seats from the less populated to the more populated areas. The right to vote still depended on a property qualification, and women remained completely excluded from the franchise. The secret ballot was introduced by the Ballot Act 1872 and, under the Corrupt and Illegal Practices Act 1883, bribery and other corrupt practices connected with elections became criminal offences.

The next extension in the franchise came in 1884 when the Franchise Act extended the vote to most male adults. Women, however, remained without the vote until 1918 when women aged 30 and over, together with all adult males, were given the vote. In 1928 the Representation of the People Act extended the suffrage to women aged 21 and over. The voting age was reduced to 18 for men and women by the Representation of the People Act 1969.

CONSTITUENCIES

FOR ELECTORAL purposes the United Kingdom is divided into geographical areas known as constituencies, each returning one member to the House of Commons. There are two types: borough and county, which are, broadly speaking, urban and rural constituencies. Their boundaries are approved by Parliament after periodic reviews conducted by boundary commissions.

Constitution and Functions of Boundary Commissions

Four separate parliamentary Boundary Commissions, constituted under the House of Commons (Redistribution of Seats) Acts 1949 and 1958, undertake periodic general reviews (at intervals of not less than 10 or more than 15 years) of constituencies in that part of the United Kingdom for which they are responsible (England, Scotland, Wales and Northern Ireland) with a view to recommending any redistribution of seats that may become necessary owing to movements of population or other causes. They may also submit interim reports on particular constituencies.

Each commission consists of the Speaker of the House of Commons as *ex officio* chairman, a judge of the High Court (or, in the case of the Commission for Scotland, a judge of the Court of Session) as deputy chairman, and two other members appointed by Government ministers. It is the usual practice for these appointments to be made after consultation with the other political parties. A Member of Parliament, other than the Speaker, cannot be a member of a boundary commission.

Assessors appointed by statute to advise the commissions are: the Registrar-General for England and Wales and the Director-General of the Ordnance Survey; the Registrar-General of Births, Deaths and Marriages in Scotland and the Director-General of the Ordnance Survey; and in Northern Ireland the Chief Electoral Officer, the Registrar-General of Births, Deaths and Marriages and the Commissioner of Valuation.

Review Procedure

There are two main stages in the review procedure. First, a commission publishes its provisional recommendations in each constituency affected, after which a month is allowed for representations to be made. The commission may then cause a local inquiry to be held, and must do so if representations are made by an interested local authority, or by 100 or more parliamentary electors in the constituency concerned. If, as a result of a local inquiry, the commission decides to alter its recommendations, the revised recommendations must also be published, but if they, also, are opposed, a further local inquiry is not obligatory. The commission must then submit a report embodying its final recommendations to the appropriate Secretary of State, who is required to submit it to Parliament with a draft Order in Council to give effect to the recommendations, with or without modifications. If modifications are proposed, the Secretary of State must at the same time present a statement of reasons for them.

The latest general reports of the commissions were submitted in 1969 and orders giving effect to their recommendations were approved by Parliament in October 1970.

The general election of February 1974 was the first to be fought on the new boundaries.

Numbers of Constituencies and Electoral Quotas

The total number of constituencies is fixed by law to provide 12 constituencies for Northern Ireland and not substantially fewer or substantially more than 613 in the rest of the United Kingdom, of which Scotland must have at least 71 and Wales at least 35. The present total number is 635 (516 in England, 71 in Scotland, 36 in Wales and 12 in Northern Ireland[1]). In making their recommendations the Boundary Commissions must, as far as possible, have regard to local government boundaries (in Northern Ireland, wards) without causing excessive disparities between the sizes of constituencies (although they are required to take account, so far as they reasonably can, of the inconvenience and breaking of local ties which may result from constituency changes). Subject to these requirements constituency electorates must be as near as is practicable to the electoral quota, a figure obtained by dividing the total electorate of that part of the United Kingdom (England, Scotland, Wales or Northern Ireland) by the number of constituencies in it at the date when the Commission begins its review.

In February 1977 the average number of electors for each constituency in England was 66,056; in Scotland, 53,336; in Wales, 57,088; and in Northern Ireland, 86,076.

---

[1] In April 1978 the Government accepted the recommendation of a Speaker's Conference that Northern Ireland parliamentary seats should be increased to 17 with the Boundary Commission having powers to vary this to 16 or 18. The change will take place after the necessary legislation has been passed by Parliament.

VOTERS AND CANDIDATES

Who May Vote

British subjects and citizens of the Irish Republic resident in the United Kingdom are entitled to vote at parliamentary elections provided that they are 18 years old, and are not subject to any legal incapacity to vote. Those eligible to vote in a particular constituency are those who were resident there on the qualifying date—10 October in England, Scotland and Wales and 15 September in Northern Ireland—for the register of electors to be used at the election, and whose names were accordingly included on the register of electors for the constituency. Provision is made for people to be registered and to vote at elections on or after the date on which they reach voting age; for this purpose, anyone reaching voting age during the currency of a register has the date of his eighteenth birthday entered on it. Commonwealth citizens are British subjects, and accordingly, if otherwise eligible, are entitled to be registered and to vote.

The register of electors is compiled annually by electoral registration officers who are employed by local government authorities in England, Scotland and Wales. In Northern Ireland the register is compiled by the Chief Electoral Officer.

In order to ascertain the names of the people in his area who are qualified to be registered, the registration officer sends each year a standard form to every separate residence in his area for completion by the occupier, or may arrange for a house-to-house canvass. Provisional electors' lists are then published and displayed (from 28 November to 16 December in England, Scotland and Wales) in such places as council offices, main post offices and public libraries. This is done to enable claims for inclusion or objections to be lodged. These are decided by the registration officer, subject to appeal in the county court or, in Scotland, the Sheriff court. The final register must be published not later than 15 February each year and comes into force on 16 February. As in the rest of the United Kingdom electors' lists in Northern Ireland first appear in November. Claims or objections must be received by 15 December; they may be allowed after examination by the Chief Electoral Officer, subject to appeal in the county court. The final register must be published by 15 February and comes into force on 16 February.

Voting in an election is voluntary.

Who May Not Vote

The following people are not entitled to vote in a parliamentary election: peers who are members of the House of Lords[1]; young people under 18 years of age; aliens; convicted offenders detained in prisons, borstals, detention centres and remand centres; and those found guilty within the previous five years of corrupt or illegal practices in connection with an election.

---

[1]Members of the House of Lords may vote in local government elections.

British Citizens Overseas

The only people not resident in the United Kingdom who are entitled to be registered as electors are Crown servants (for instance, embassy or consular officials), members of the armed forces, the staff of the British Council, and their spouses if living abroad with their husbands or wives. These voters are collectively known as 'service voters' and are registered by making individual 'service declarations' and sending them to the registration officer of their home constituency. If they are unable to give an address at which they would have been residing in the United Kingdom on the next qualifying date but for the circumstances of their service, they may give an address at which they formerly resided.

British subjects who are on the electoral register and who are temporarily abroad on business may vote by proxy if they cannot return in time for polling day; those who are away from home on holiday cannot vote. British subjects, other than service voters, living abroad are not entitled to be registered and therefore cannot vote.

How Votes are Cast

In parliamentary elections, each elector may cast one vote, and generally does so in person at the particular polling station allotted to him in his constituency. Service voters may vote by proxy, but if they are in the United Kingdom at the time of the election they may vote either in person, by post or by proxy. Certain other people who have good reason for not being able to attend at a polling station (for instance, on grounds of religious observance, or because of physical incapacity, nature of occupation or change of address) may, after application, cast their vote by post.

Candidates

Any man or woman who is not disqualified from voting may offer himself as a candidate at a parliamentary election for any constituency provided that he has reached the age of 21. Undischarged bankrupts, clergymen of the Church of England, Church of Scotland, Church of Ireland and Roman Catholic Church, and people holding certain other offices are, however, not eligible. The House of Commons Disqualification Act 1975 defines those who may not become members of Parliament. They include: holders of judicial office; civil servants; members of the armed forces; policemen and policewomen; holders of a wide range of public posts—for instance, in public corporations and Government commissions; and members of the legislature of any country or territory outside the Commonwealth.

A candidate is usually a member of one of the main national political parties. Smaller political parties and groups also nominate candidates, and individuals may be nominated without party support. It is not necessary for a candidate to be resident in the constituency for which he stands.

Candidates, other than independent candidates, are selected by the political party constituency association through its selection committee which interviews possible candidates and decides which one to adopt. The Labour and Conservative national party organisations, for example, maintain lists of approved candidates from which constituency associations may make a choice, but the latter are free to select someone not on the approved list; once selected, the candidate has to be approved by the national party organisation before being adopted as the 'prospective' candidate for the constituency. Between the time of adoption and the opening of the election campaign, candidates make themselves known to voters in the constituency and involve themselves with local affairs.

Candidates may vote in their constituencies, provided that they are on the electoral register.

ELECTORAL PROCEDURE

ELECTORAL procedure in the United Kingdom is based principally on the Representation of the People Acts 1949 and 1969.

Royal Proclamations and Election Writs

When it has been decided to dissolve a Parliament, orders are made by the Queen in Council directing the Lord Chancellor and the Secretary of State for Northern Ireland (a) to affix the Great Seal to the royal proclamation for dissolving the old and calling the new Parliament, and (b) to issue the Writs of Election (which are thereupon issued from the Office of the Clerk of the Crown in Chancery[1]). When a by-election is to be held, the writ is issued on the Speaker's warrant to the Clerk of the Crown.

For a general election, the writs are issued as soon as practicable after the issue of the proclamation summoning the new Parliament—usually on the same day; for a by-election, as soon as possible after the issue of the warrant.

Administration of Elections

In England and Wales the Home Office (in Scotland, the Scottish Home and Health Department and in Northern Ireland the Northern Ireland Office) is responsible for the general oversight of electoral law. The conduct of an election in an English or Welsh constituency is the responsibility of the returning officer in that constituency (the sheriff of the county, the mayor of a London borough or, outside Greater London, the chairman of a district council). However, most of the duties are carried out by the registration officer as acting returning officer or any deputy whom he may appoint. In Scotland, there are no acting returning officers and the statutory returning officer is responsible for the entire conduct of the election. The Returning Officers (Scotland) Act 1977 provides for returning officers for regional and islands councils also to be returning officers for Parliamentary elections in Scotland. The returning officer is normally the chief executive or the director of administration of the regional or islands council. In Northern Ireland the Chief Electoral Officer appoints full-time deputies as acting returning officers.

The returning or acting returning officer publishes the notice of election (which also gives the date on which the poll will be held should there be a contest) and the nominations; sends an official poll card (which sets out the name of the constituency, the elector's name, address and number on the register. the place of the elector's polling station and the date and hours of the poll) to all electors in the constituency; arranges for the printing of the ballot papers; sees that there are enough polling stations; provides the ballot boxes and other necessary equipment in the polling stations and ensures that each station is properly arranged with compartments to safeguard the secrecy of the vote; appoints and pays the necessary staff at polling stations (a presiding officer and a certain number of poll clerks); and makes arrangements for the counting of votes.

The official expenses of a parliamentary election are paid by the Treasury.

---

[1] In Northern Ireland, from the Office of the Clerk of the Crown for Northern Ireland.

Nomination of Candidates

Each candidate must be nominated on the prescribed nomination paper, which must state in full his name and home address. It may also include a political or personal description not exceeding six words in length, although this is not obligatory. The nomination paper must be signed by two electors as proposer and seconder, and by eight other electors.

A candidate must consent to his nomination in writing.

For general elections, nomination papers must be delivered between the hours of 10.00 and 15.00 (on Saturday, between those of 10.00 and 12.00) on any day after the publication of the notice of election, but not later than the eighth day after the date of the proclamation summoning the new Parliament. For a by-election delivery is the same as for a general election, except that the last day is fixed by the returning officer and must be:

(a)   in a county constituency, not earlier than the fourth day after the publication of the notice of election, nor later than the ninth day after that on which the writ is received; and

(b)   in a borough[1] constituency, not earlier than the third day after the date of the publication of the notice of election, nor later than the seventh day after that on which the writ is received.

The candidate, or someone on his behalf, has to deposit the sum of £150 with the returning officer at the place, and during the time, for delivery of nomination papers. If the candidate polls at least one-eighth (12·5 per cent) of the total votes cast, he is entitled to have his deposit returned; if not, his deposit is forfeit. The deposit is intended to ensure that the candidate is a serious contestant.

A candidate may withdraw from the election within the time for the delivery of nomination papers, but no later. The notice of withdrawal must be signed by the candidate and attested by one witness and delivered to the returning officer.

At, or before, the latest time for the delivery of nomination papers the name and address of the election agent (see p 10) of each candidate must be declared to the returning officer.

Objections to nominations (which need not be in writing) may be lodged with the returning officer during the hours allowed on the last day for delivery of nominations and the hour following, and, if the last day is a Saturday, between the hours of 13.00 and 15.00 of the day before. The returning officer decides on the validity of the objections. The persons entitled to object to the validity of a nomination paper are some of those entitled to attend nominations—that is to say, the candidate, his election agent, his proposer and seconder; but the husband or wife of a candidate, although entitled to attend nominations, is not entitled to object.

At the close of the time for making objections, or as soon as possible after any objections are disposed of, the returning officer publishes the names of the candidates nominated, with those of the proposers and seconders.

---

[1]'Burgh' in Scotland.

Polling Day

At a general election, all polling must take place on the ninth day after the last day for delivery of nomination papers. For a by-election, the day is fixed by the returning officer not earlier than the seventh, nor later than the ninth, day after the last day for delivery of nomination papers.

If a candidate dies between the publication of nominations and the poll, or after the poll has begun and before the result is declared, proceedings begin afresh as if the writ had been received 28 days after the returning officer had received proof of death.

Time-table

The time-table for a general election is:

(1) royal proclamation;

(2) issue of writs, as soon as practicable after the royal proclamation;

(3) publication of the Notice of Election, not later than the second day after that on which the writ is received;

(4) delivery of nomination papers, not later than the eighth day after the royal proclamation; and

(5) polling day, on the ninth day after the last day for delivery of nomination papers.

In computing any period of time for the purposes of the time-table, Sundays, the periods beginning with the last week-day before and ending with the first week-day after the recognised Christmas, Easter and other bank holiday periods, or any days appointed for public thanksgiving or mourning, are disregarded. There are slight variations in the time-table for by-elections.

The Election Campaign

At the start of the election campaign, the candidate normally sends out a printed election address, stating his policy. During the campaign his time is spent in canvassing householders, addressing people in the streets and holding public meetings explaining and commending the policies of his party. He also meets various sections of the community who may wish to know his views on policy affecting their particular interests. Throughout the campaign he acts on the advice of his agent.

The Election Agent

Each parliamentary candidate appoints an election agent[1] who is responsible for the conduct of the campaign and, in particular, for the control of expenses. The agent, who should be familiar with election law and practice, must be appointed on, or before, nomination day and the appointment must be declared to the returning officer; if the agent is anyone other than the candidate the declaration must be made by the agent or accompanied by a written note of acceptance by him. The agent may act without payment or he

---

[1]Candidates may act as their own agent but normally choose not to do so.

may be paid a fee which must be included in the maximum amount permitted for a candidate's expenses.

A candidate's election agent may also employ paid polling agents, clerks and messengers within the limits of his election expenses, and any number of unpaid polling agents and other voluntary helpers for canvassing, public speaking and clerical work.

Committee Rooms

When the writ marking the start of an election is received, the election agent arranges for a number of committee rooms to be available. These must not be premises licensed for the sale of alcohol. Committee rooms are used by the party organisation as headquarters for speakers, canvassers, messengers and others concerned in the election campaign, for keeping the candidate supplied with the latest news and developments in the political scene to assist him in his speeches and canvassing, and for sending out election addresses and leaflets.

Printing and Advertising

All orders for printing and advertising must be given by the candidate or his agent. Unauthorised persons are guilty of corrupt practice if they incur expenses in issuing advertisements and other publicity material for the purpose of promoting or procuring the election of a candidate. The name and address of the printer and publisher must be on all bills, leaflets and similar material and no payment must be made or offered for exhibiting them, unless to an advertising agent in the ordinary course of business.

Public Meetings

A candidate may hold as many public meetings as he chooses and may invite other speakers, including the leading members of his party, to speak in his support. Meetings may be held out of doors, provided they are conducted in an orderly manner and do not cause obstruction, and indoors—in halls and other suitable premises. In England, Scotland and Wales a candidate is entitled to the use of schools or public meeting rooms in the constituency at reasonable times during the election campaign. In Northern Ireland candidates may not use schools or meeting rooms maintained out of public funds.

All who take part in an election must, in all they may say or write, conform to the ordinary laws of the land regarding defamation. The defence of qualified privilege (that the defamatory statement could be proved to be accurate and not inspired by malice) is not applicable to candidates' election addresses.

Broadcasting

Arrangements for party election broadcasts during a general election are made by a committee comprising political parties, the British Broadcasting Corporation (BBC) and the Independent Broadcasting Authority (IBA). Television election broadcasts are relayed simultaneously by all channels. The agreed allocation of broadcasts for the October 1974 general election gave the Labour and Conservative parties five television broadcasts of ten minutes each and seven radio broadcasts (four of ten minutes and three of five minutes), while the Liberal party had four television broadcasts of ten minutes and five radio broadcasts (three of ten minutes and two of five minutes). In Scotland the Scottish National Party had two television and two radio broadcasts, each lasting ten minutes. In Wales Plaid Cymru (Welsh Nationalists) had one television and one radio broadcast, each lasting ten minutes. Other parties with more than 50 candidates may also receive some television and radio time: during the October 1974 election campaign, the National Front had one broadcast on television and one on radio, each lasting five minutes. In all these broadcasts the editorial control is with the parties. The broadcasting authorities also each arrange a series of regional programmes which include, on a basis of parity, representatives of parties with candidates in at least 20 per cent of the constituencies within the region.

During the election, the BBC and IBA also broadcast general programmes about the election and news reports on the progress of the election campaign. Under the Representation of the People Act 1969, a candidate cannot take part in a programme about his constituency during an election campaign if any of his rivals neither takes part nor consents to its going forward.

The use for election propaganda of any transmitting stations outside the United Kingdom is prohibited except in pursuance of arrangements made with the BBC or IBA (or a programme contractor).

Election Expenses

The expenses a candidate may incur are strictly regulated by law, any infringement of which may involve severe penalties, including the annulment of the election if the winning candidate is concerned.

The maximum expenditure which may be incurred by a candidate is:

(a) in borough constituencies, £1,075, plus 6p for every eight entries in the register of electors;

(b) in county constituencies, £1,075, plus 6p for every six entries in the register.

A candidate may send by post one communication relating to the election (this is usually his election address), free of postal charge, to every elector in his constituency, provided that it does not weigh more than 57 grammes (two ounces). All other expenses, apart from the candidate's personal expenses, including fees to the election agent, printing and stationery, advertising and bill-posting, the hire of rooms for committee rooms and public meetings, and the employment of a secretary, must be covered by the statutory sums. No expenses for the election of a candidate may be incurred by anyone other than the candidate himself, the election agent or a person authorised by the agent. After the election, the agent must make a return of all election expenses to the returning officer within 35 days of the poll.

Corrupt and Illegal Practices

Certain offences connected with elections, if committed by the candidate or his agent, or with his knowledge and consent, will render his election void. These offences are divided into: (1) corrupt practices, including bribery, treating, undue influence, personation (voting as some other person), and false declarations concerning election expenses; and (2) illegal practices, including illegal payments, illegal employment, illegal hiring of conveyances or premises, improper conduct of the election campaign, various voting offences, and breaches of the law governing election expenses.

Anyone guilty of corrupt or illegal practices at elections is liable to criminal prosecution and, on conviction, to penalties of imprisonment or fine.

The Poll

Each constituency is divided into a number of polling districts. In each district there is a designated polling place where the polling station is situated.

The ballot is secret, and the only people allowed in the polling station are the presiding officer (who is in charge), the polling clerks, the police on duty, the candidates, the candidates' election agents and polling agents, and such number of electors as the presiding officer may decide to admit at any one time. All those concerned with the poll, except the police officer on duty, must previously have made a 'declaration of secrecy' before the returning officer, a justice of the peace or certain other persons.

The hours of poll are 7.00 to 22.00. Just before the poll opens, the presiding officer shows the ballot boxes to those at the polling station to prove that the boxes are empty. He then locks and seals them.

On entering the polling station, the voter is directed to the presiding officer or poll clerk who asks the voter his name, checks that it is on the register, and places a mark against the entry in the register. This indicates that the voter has received a ballot paper but does not show the particular ballot paper he has received. (The officer or clerk also marks the voter's number on the counterfoil.) The ballot paper is marked by the officer or clerk with an official mark which perforates the ballot paper. It is then detached and handed to the voter. The official mark is necessary to eliminate the chances of forged ballot papers being placed in the ballot box.

The voter then goes to a booth which is screened to maintain secrecy and marks his paper with a cross opposite the name of the candidate of his choice. He folds the paper to conceal his vote and puts it into the ballot box. The paper lists the candidates alphabetically in the order of their surnames; it also contains a brief description of each candidate indicating his or her occupation and political party.

A paper spoiled by mistake must be returned to the presiding officer who, if satisfied the spoiling was inadvertent, gives another and cancels the first, but does not destroy it. At the close of the poll the presiding officer must make a packet of any such spoilt papers and deliver it to the returning officer. A person who is unable to read, or is physically incapacitated, may have his ballot paper marked for him by the presiding officer. A blind person may, alternatively, be assisted to vote by a companion.

The poll must not be closed before the statutory time for any temporary purpose—for instance, an adjournment for lunch. After that time no votes can be accepted except from voters who have already received ballot papers, and, once closed, the poll cannot be reopened. Before the ballot boxes are removed from the polling station they are sealed to prevent the introduction of additional ballot papers. In the presence of the candidates' agents, the presiding officer makes up into packets to which he affixes his seal (the polling agents may also affix seals on behalf of the candidates):

(1) the ballot box unopened but with the key attached;

(2) the unused and spoilt ballot papers;

(3) the tendered votes list, that is to say, the list of voters whose ballot papers have been endorsed by the presiding officer—for instance, voters who have used 'tendered' ballot papers,[1] blind voters assisted by companions, and voters whose votes have been recorded by the presiding officer because of their physical incapacity or their inability to read; and

(4) the marked copy of the register of voters, the counterfoils of the used ballot papers, and the certificates as to polling staff and policemen on duty at the station.

These packets are then delivered by him or by some other approved person to the returning officer together with a statement (known as the ballot paper account) showing the number of ballot papers entrusted to him, and accounting for them under the headings of 'ballot papers issued and not otherwise accounted for', and 'unused', 'spoilt', and 'tendered' ballot papers.

Postal Voting

A postal ballot paper, together with a 'declaration of identity', a ballot paper envelope and a return postal envelope is sent to a person entitled to vote by post as soon as practicable. Apart from the returning officer and his staff, a candidate or his agent may be present at the issue and receipt of postal ballot papers. Special postal ballot boxes are provided for the receipt of the return postal envelope which should contain the declaration of identity, properly completed, and the sealed ballot paper envelope with the ballot paper inside. The boxes are locked and sealed by the returning officer, and those agents who wish to affix their seal. These ballot boxes are opened in the presence of the agents. The outer envelopes are opened, and the declarations of identity checked against the ballot paper envelopes. Special receptacles are provided for the declarations of identity and for the ballot paper envelopes, and special procedures are followed to prevent abuse of the system. If all is well, the ballot paper envelopes are then opened and the postal ballot papers are placed in a locked and sealed ballot box, which thereafter is treated like any other ordinary ballot box in the count.

---

[1] A tendered ballot paper is one issued to a person claiming to be a particular elector named in the register after another person making the same claim has already voted. Instead of being put into the ballot box, it must be given to the presiding officer, endorsed by him with the voter's name and number in the register, and set aside in a separate packet. The voter's name and his number in the register must be entered on a 'tendered votes list'.

Postal ballot papers are indistinguishable to the naked eye from other ballot papers, although they bear a different perforation mark. They are mixed with the other ballot papers before they are finally counted.

The Count

The votes must be counted as soon as practicable after the poll at a place chosen by the returning officer. In addition to the returning officer and his staff, the following persons have the right to be present at the count: the candidates (and husbands or wives), the candidates' election agents and their counting agents. (Each candiate may appoint counting agents before the beginning of the poll. The number of these, which must be the same for each candidate, may be limited by the returning officer. They observe the counting of the votes and check for errors.) Other visitors (including the broadcasting authorities) may attend only if the returning officer is satisfied, if possible after consulting the election agents, that the official counting of the votes will not be impeded. After examination of the seals, the ballot boxes are opened and emptied, and the total number of papers in each box is counted. The ballot paper account is then verified in the presence of the election agents and thereafter the papers are mixed together and sorted according to the candidates for whom they are marked.

The counting assistants usually work in pairs in the presence of the candidates' agents. Doubtful papers are put aside, and it is the duty of the returning officer to decide upon their validity.

When voting is very close, a candidate or his election agent may ask for a re-count, or further re-counts. This request may be granted at the returning officer's discretion.

If the number of votes cast for the leading candidates is equal, the result is decided by lot.

The returning officer must then declare the result of the poll. The declaration is usually made publicly—for instance, from a balcony outside the hall or place where the count is made. The time between the close of the poll and the announcement of the result varies from constituency to constituency. The majority of results are known within five or six hours of the close of poll while the remainder, chiefly in rural constituencies, are usually declared the day after polling day.

If the candidate elected is alleged to be disqualified or to have committed malpractices, the returning officer nevertheless declares him to be elected and then leaves the objector to seek his remedy by election petition (see below).

When the election is over, deposits of those candidates who have polled more than 12·5 per cent of the total poll are returned to them.

Election Petitions

Any person wishing to question the conduct or result of an election must do so by presenting an election petition. In England and Wales election petitions are presented to the High Court in the Queen's Bench Division. In Scotland they are presented to the Court of Session and in Northern Ireland to the High Court in the Queen's Bench Division.

The petitioner must have been either an elector or a candidate in the election. The petition must be made in the prescribed form, and must state the facts and grounds of the complaint. The petition is tried by two judges sitting in open court without a jury and, except in special circumstances, the hearing must take place within the constituency concerned. If a successful candidate is found by an election court to be personally guilty, or guilty through his agent, of any corrupt or illegal practice, then his election is void. The election may also be held void for other reasons—for instance, because the candidate was not qualified or because of serious irregularities in the conduct of the election which are likely to have affected its result.

APPENDIX 1

THE GENERAL ELECTION OF OCTOBER 1974

The last general election was held on 10 October 1974 when the Labour Party gained a majority of three seats over all other parties. The total number of electors entitled to vote was just over 40 million and 72·8 per cent cast their votes. The table below shows the number of seats and votes obtained by each party[1]:

	Seats	Votes cast
Labour	319	11,468,136
Conservative	276	10,428,970
Liberal	13	5,346,800
Scottish National	11	839,628
United Ulster Unionist Coalition	10	407,778
Plaid Cymru (Welsh Nationalists)	3	166,321
Social Democratic and Labour (Northern Ireland)	1	154,193
Independent (Northern Ireland)	1	32,795
The Speaker[2]	1	35,705
Others[3]	0	308,280
	635	29,188,606

[1]As a result of subsequent by-elections, the resignation of two Labour members in 1976 to sit as Scottish Labour Party members, and the dissolution of the United Ulster Unionist Coalition in May 1977, the distribution of seats in the House of Commons in mid-May 1978 was: Labour 306, Conservative 282, Liberal 13, Scottish National 11, Official Unionist (Northern Ireland) 7, Plaid Cymru 3, Independent Unionists (Northern Ireland) 2, Scottish Labour 2, Democratic Unionist (Northern Ireland) 1, Independent (Northern Ireland) 1, Social Democratic and Labour (Northern Ireland) 1 and Vacancies 2. Not included are the Speaker and his three deputies (the Chairman of Ways and Means and the first and second Deputy Chairmen of Ways and Means) who do not vote except in their official capacity in the event of a tie.

[2]The Speaker presides over the debates of the House of Commons and enforces the observance of all rules for preserving order during the proceedings. He is elected by the House of Commons and, once elected, may stand for his constituency as the Speaker seeking re-election.

[3]Including the National Front, the Communist Party of Great Britain, various Northern Irish political groups and independent candidates.

APPENDIX 2

GENERAL ELECTION RESULTS 1945–74

The table below shows the results of the ten general elections held between 1945 and 1974. Redistribution of seats place took in 1950, 1955 and 1974. The table gives separate figures for the Labour, Conservative and Liberal parties; the category 'others' includes the Scottish National Party, Plaid Cymru, the Communist Party of Great Britain, the National Front, some political groups in Northern Ireland, and independent candidates.

	Seats won	Votes cast	Percentage share of total vote
1945			
Labour	393	11,992,292	48·0
Conservative and Associates	212	9,945,796	39·8
Liberal[1]	12	2,245,319	9·0
Others[2]	23	795,542	3·2
1950			
Labour	315	13,295,736	46·4
Conservative and Associates	298	12,501,983	43·5
Liberal[1]	9	2,621,489	9·1
Others[2]	3	350,269	1·0
1951			
Conservative and Associates	321	13,724,418	48·0
Labour	295	13,948,385	48·8
Liberal[1]	6	730,551	2·5
Others	3	198,969	0·7
1955			
Conservative and Associates	344	13,285,519	49·7
Labour	277	12,405,254	46·3
Liberal[1]	6	722,402	2·7
Others[2]	3	346,554	1·3
1959			
Conservative and Associates	365	13,750,875	49·4
Labour	258	12,216,172	43·8
Liberal[1]	6	1,640,760	5·9
Others	1	254,845	0·9
1964			
Labour	317	12,205,812	44·1
Conservative and Associates	303	11,981,047	43·3
Liberal[1]	9	3,101,106	11·2
Others[2]	1	369,183	1·4
1966			
Labour	363	13,066,173	47·9
Conservative and Associates	253	11,418,455	41·9
Liberal[1]	12	2,327,457	8·6
Others[2]	2	452,669	1·6

	Seats won	Votes cast	Percentage share of total vote
1970			
Conservative and Associates	330	13,145,123	46·4
Labour	287	12,179,341	43·0
Liberal[1]	6	2,117,035	7·5
Others[2]	7	903,299	3·1
1974 (February)			
Labour	301	11,654,726	37·2
Conservative	296	11,924,755	38·1
Liberal[1]	14	6,063,470	19·3
Others[2]	24	1,690,275	5·4
1974 (October)			
Labour	319	11,468,136	39·3
Conservative	276	10,428,970	35·7
Liberal[1]	13	5,346,800	18·3
Others[2]	27	1,944,700	6·6

Source: *The Times* Guides to the House of Commons.

---

[1]The number of seats contested by the Liberal Party varied considerably in the elections and this is partly the reason for the fluctuations in the party's vote.

[2]Including the Speaker of the House of Commons.

READING LIST

			£
BUTLER, D. E. *and* SLOMAN, ANNE. British Political Facts 1900–1975. Fourth edition. ISBN 0 333 17838 6.	*Macmillan*	1975	15·00
BUTLER, D. E. *and* KAVANAGH, DENNIS. The British General Election of February 1974. ISBN 0 333 17297 3.	*Macmillan*	1974	5·95
——The British General Election of October 1974. ISBN 0 333 18053 4.	*Macmillan*	1975	10·00
BUTLER, D. E. *and* STOKES, DONALD. Political Change in Britain. Basis of Electoral Choice.			
ISBN 0 333 15239 5 (hardback).	*Macmillan*	1975	15·00
ISBN 0 333 22600 3 (paperback).		1977	4·95
CRAIG, F. W. S. (*Editor*). British Parliamentary Election Statistics 1918–1970. ISBN 0 900178 04 3.	*Macmillan*	1971	3·75
TEER, FRANK *and* SPENCE, JAMES D. Political Opinion Polls. ISBN 0 09 115230 5.	*Hutchinson*	1973	3·50
European Assembly Elections Act 1978 ISBN 0 10 541078 0	*HMSO*	1978	0·40
The Times Guide to the House of Commons, October 1974. ISBN 0 7230 0124 3.	*The Times*	1974	7·00
Report of the Committee on Financial Aid to Political Parties. Cmnd 6601. ISBN 0 10 166010 3.	*HMSO*	1976	4·05
Representation of the People Act 1949. ISBN 0 10 850063 2.	*HMSO*	Reprinted 1975	3·50
Representation of the People Act 1969. ISBN 0 10 541569 3.	*HMSO*	1969	0·22½
The British Parliament. COI reference pamphlet. ISBN 0 11 700779 X.	*HMSO*	1975	1·50
The Organisation of Political Parties in Britain. COI reference paper, R4769.	*COI*	1977	0·36

Printed in England for Her Majesty's Stationery Office by Ebenezer Baylis & Son Ltd, The Trinity Press, Worcester, and London
Dd. 555499 K32 6/78 3735